Cloud Fire

KATHERINE HASTINGS

SPUYTEN DUYVIL

New York City

Library of Congress Cataloging-in-Publication Data

Hastings, Katherine.
Cloud Fire / Katherine Hastings.
p. cm.
ISBN 978-1-881471-11-0
I. Title.
PS3608.A86145C58 2012
811'.6--dc23
2012018785

For Cathy

TABLE OF CONTENTS

Fog knows
 what love isn't —
  an erasing of existence

Cloud Fire

CLOUDS

We begin by christening them — salt grains
of sky rising rhythmically from the soft
nursery of fog. *Moth-winged nebula.*

Haloed pillar of snow. Feather and float.
Pasture and jaw. Infinitesimal star birth
times a million. They are poured milk we spoon

and swallow, wear like skin. They polish our
cheeks and stiffen our fingers. They rest on our
tongues and together we taste them gliding

over the wide water, silver in foglight.
We cannot fly but nest ourselves in clouds.
But for the slow voyaging mist, we feel naked.

We do this like children or angels living
on the ledges of waves and lips, downy
wings so white they hum every color.

Bees rolling in a white rose.

My city whose hair is a cloud fire
Whose dreams are tumbleweeds of mist
Whose body is a ladder from barnacle to night star
Whose mouth bares the fragrance of the white-flecked sea
Whose tongue is of onyx and humming wires

My city whose streams are rock doves and parrots
Whose bright arm is a springboard for love and suicides
Whose heart is filled with winsome flowering kisses
Whose lap is a playground of canvas swings
Whose ghost stands behind them pushing them, pushing them

up from the silver portal of heaven
into the silver portal of heaven

Clouds brush a language of shadow and light.
Waves speak their own tongue of dissolution;
spindly-legged birds rushing their ruffled edges
dip into the shore's sweet pockets and swallow.

We walk along the back-and forth of it all —
sand dollars and wood, seaweed and jellies —
heads down, measuring the exact breadth of

every word. For a moment, our history
of who is correct and who is right is stamped
into the cool ground and the wind we've

walked through so many times, aslant, is more
like a laying on of hands than wind. If there is
anything more to be said, we don't know what it is.

So we listen to the sea, to the clouds, to the bubbles
that rise from the deep and burst the last word.
It was always theirs anyway.

The sun that day
        The arched bridge
    The sea   lit from the deep
        Sorcery
Two Untamed Angels flying impulsively
    from sudden cliffs
their spiral
        spiral
                into the wind's
silken stimulus

Curious spark chamber
        of movement
of fingered wings
        blended honey-flow
                (alive!)
seaweed   sun   arched bridge   shoreline
        lips   lips   and legs
music
        husky and howling

Only the smallest leaves
move
slightly in their dreams

Streams play on stones —
everything sings

Even faded colors hum
in rock-walled gardens

The sun closes its eye
on the way to the sea
The sea

pleasures seabirds
between its teeth

Bubbles of music rise
to the rotating sky

The moon has everything under a spell

January is a song
composed of mist
and caesura

Now and then, a cloud leaf placidly breaks
from the cerulean flow of sky water.

It lowers itself through tree limbs, reaches
into the stark whiteness of your bones.

Swept into the hollow of the moment
you feel far into that moist body adrift.

A vision, wind-combed, waits at the edge
of red horizon, a sea of echoes

emanates from the intermittent moon,
veil, moon. It means nothing if not the

opening and closing of desire,
as a flower formed of fog floats through,

is gone, leaving only your conscience
forever whirling in the breeze.

Bright day over the far-reaching heave,
       low drift through Mayacama valley,
              a scene of snow without snow

Fog-mantle on the breast of meadow
       where voices from the emerald womb —
              feathered throats and bud bloom — sing through

A slow ship on the field among flocks and fences
A swathing garment of mystical moistness wends and wends
              under stars appearing, disappearing

Hands hold what will be held, or with the heft of emptiness
       wait restlessly for some wild, sudden wind to turn them
              into birds tumultuously winging

O ecstatic girl, your toes in the grass, your hair a world bursting!
       Under the sun you leap into the low cloud-drift, sing
              I am here! I am here! A thousand droplets kissing

Where are you shiny girl, so new to human-hood?
       With your wide open eyes, red shoes skipping through
this odd, marvelous and ancient world — Where?

White vespers. Fog suspends, enters
smooth-coated and swift, swings
the deep bell of the bay.

The city rises into it, lips
half-open

> *Come to me voiceless as snow,*
> *majestic river flowing*
> *Shape my nights*
> *Dream-float through me*
> *as the evening star shines through*
> *to find the woman there*

> *Silver melt of sorrow's opposite,*
> *brush my waiting beneath the cypress*
> *cleaved and swept, perpetually*
> *receiving. Hold open your palm*
> *Droplets gather fragrance from the shore*
> *Torrential mist!*
> *You are the poetry and the tongue*
> *of my hills*

(Arrival)

The field was topaz-colored,
the bay a chilled diamond sheet.
We walked along through breeze and spray,
the gray sky drummed a beat.
Migration of stork and crane.

Harbor seals swept past thrush and wigeon.
The vista rippled — even the lone fan of rain
that never reached, and the sun's red stain.

(Iridescence)

The world breathed a breath, the moon began.
The year was done with Death, his greedy hand.
No more apparitions making gestures
upon the wind-combed sand.

(Departure)

The moon drew the bay to sea.
The mud flats snapped with life.
Shore birds ran in regiments calling
Peep! Petite ballerinas laying charts
of starlight at our feet.

The low gray sky is living. Cool clouds loll
and roll into soft shapes — migrating bears.
Foghorns call.

Their song has two notes — a rise, a fall.
Haunting pairs that drape us
in silver-wingéd shawls.

We dream-walk, hesitate and stall
to feel the tingle on our skin — soft, salty air
billowed from the sea over the old brick wall.

Mist floats past the steeples of Peter and Paul.
It has floated for hundreds of years.
We are the world's disintegrating dolls

let loose from red/black halls
into experience — hearts burning like flares.
The fog moves in, covers us, and dares.

Come dusk, at the minute the two-toned horn
blows under the bridge the music of fog
and upturned collars — a collaboration
of wisp and wool — when sea merges with sky —
the cool with the warm — the chapel of memory
lights its lamps. A young girl kneels to barnacles
and bat rays, dogs run higgledy-piggledy
on the green, fishermen chug west, alone.
Only a few memories tempt destruction —
a type of forgiveness is oft required.

Imagine a schoolgirl in June — a bird lifting
into the small opening of blue, leaving every scrap
of darkness behind — hallways, blankets and eyes —
one city light for each star burning new.

Cloud angels dress as flames,
fly the birthyard for boatmen and bells
Foghorns blow their low slow song
into the mouth of vocation

Wavelets
fold and fall   fold and fall
It's every child for herself
said the dead man to the living girl

It wasn't the moon she saw on his tongue
but a prison left crazy with turnkeys
Intricate lunation

Inside the clouds are trumpet vines and red
bougainvillea spangling the walls.
Over the bay on golden hills, the dead
grasses, green in winter, crisp by fall.

Children scamper within the roiling mist,
brightly colored jackets bleed through gray.
Each dandelion is a star shed, or fallen kiss
whose seeds are held to lips, blown away

like small balloons into the world's silvered hair
falling in waves on the city's crested breast —
flower-foamed, blue-grained, unraveling air.
Love and grief moil nakedly — phosphoresce.

It's the sigh of leaves,
the silver ripples in the stream.
Though the apples on the hills
are erased by vines —
the waving blossoms gone —
golden grass still threads the dawn.

Fog feathers by in wingéd wisps
beneath the cradling oaks
until the wide-sky day,
drawn dark to Bodega's Irish rim,
slips to sea in crimson bars —
our home crowned with sudden stars.

Foglight, there is a mystery about thee —
a silent heavenish thing
risen from the sea in waves
of ghostly wings

It is light —
the air upon the breast
is angel breath — sweet
among the shadows
of love's slant universe

On the road to Kirby Cove
        blackbirds and ravens
sea wind everywhere

Dream light imaginings
        are sprung here
Wings lift at will,
release the torture that tears
        as fire tears

After many years and many changes
I return and return to sea mist —
        her lips on me, her touch
shimmer down my frame of flying forms —
        rainbow winged

Here is merriment,
        the leap at the gate where salt
sponges up memories — insphered —
of the grieving girl, squeezes them out
        at the edge of the world
until like an exhalation
the world drops through altered wind,
gathers all light that heals the wound

Beyond the blue bay day
the fertile field of moon-filled sleep
        — silver beamed —
will lie under the stars
        as a flower lives
        folded by night

Pushing off from the wall
Andante con moto
cool water silks through wing of hair
against face, breasts, legs —
Andante espressivo
every millimeter between them

Watery flight over a city
constructed of one long block — perfect green tiles miles below
Molto allegro
White cells of water, jewel-lined
undulate amoeba-shapes over
white empty roadways
Andante sustenuto

Rainbow, rainbow

Arms lift and enter the surface,
Poco agitato
trace arcs through silvery light,
pull the body forward into the feel
of water
Andante tranquillo

Water music plays with and between each breath —
Allegretto grazioso
songs without words

RED CHAIR AT THE EDGE

Comfort here — a belonging to —
white-crowned songs carried by waves
crescendo/decrescendo
        murmur-crawl across sand
                                there
where memories are etched
        stippled

        O friend, washed out to sea
        Your name comes back to me
                with grief

Under the honey-sun
each fleck of foam doubles
to angel wings

Pelicans snare for deep pockets
fish silver-satin'd

The sea, an opus
comes from sky —
an extension of

        You called in sick that day
        Cast your line from rocks
        Dinner, say,
        one for each

        How thrilled the blue calm stolen hours
                and then the slapdown
                the mangle the

                    pull
                              pull
                                        pull
to the operatic end
          lamentable breath/unbreath
reduced to a line of ink

Red chair at the edge, old notebook
absence-filled

Dogs run with wind on their backs, spines limber
into arches and eights, unable to stop their exclamations,
loops. They struggle to juggle
ball, bird, kelp, crab,
dead thing, oh yum dead thing   More!

          The cold wave caught him like an abusive lover
          swept him skin-loosed

                    o dead nest o deep

          All these years
          I release
          I release you
          Take out the "I"
          and there you go

Wind awakes
blows birds across the world
ruffles the closing bud of day

Licks throat

This red-chaired playhouse
is flesh
is fed on
is fed

S. F. Bref

Sea fog, come through my gates of cabled gold
where nets once hung to catch any man who
flew. (They formed a club called Halfway to Hell!)
Cover me coldly with your blue-born breast.

My thousand eyes will greet you as fairies
do — many-colored and feathered. The bell
on the Bay will sway over shadowed waves,
announce your entrance with crystalline breath.

I am your queen waiting with skyward curves.
My body arcs up for you over old
treasure chests buried under black paved bones.
I have been loved before, sometimes to death.

Are my hills too high? My valleys too bold?
Climb me, fill me sea fog, where others fail.

Note: The bref double is an "odd" French, syllabic form
consisting of 3 quatrains and a final couplet, making 14 lines.
Unlike a sonnet, however, it has three rhymes — the first two
appearing twice in the first three quatrains, all of which end with
the third rhyme. There are also 5 unrhymed lines.

INGREDIENTS FOR FOG SOUP

One love-carved bench, back swallowed.
Two children, arms outstretched and missing.
Bare skin (as much as possible) kissed by mist.
A long sprinkle of falling stars.

One large sponge of silence.
An absence of shade and shine.
One bridge, and one city, gone.
One memory haunting as the dead.

A magician with white hair.

WHITE CROW

This little crow wears a coat of snow.
Shaking like a pup, his *up*
feels the weight of light.

His wings, his feathered chest, are blank
as morning stars erased. His eyes
shards of night through the low fog flow.

Mottled bud of shroud and cloud,
he flashes onyx —
is gone

Field Song

The body lifted towards the sun, opened and
opened away from itself, arms spread to air,
expanded, full of light and atmosphere soft
against belly and breast. The body cooled in the air.
Every pore filled with the scent of nature transforming —
pine needles in the rain, mushrooms pushing up
through dark — all the sweetness of decay and birth.

Blood heat   Blood sleep

To open one's body, finally, to sail swiftly over
the blue-green planet, to fill one's arms with light
though small pulsing anchors prick and prick,
earthbound in their bondage of grief. Look! Outward!
The face is open with a full expression of energy,
relieved. The body flies upward, soars as if it would
mend in weightlessness, openness.

My love, if I die and you don't…

The white moon sinks into the sea.
Shadows and deer graze side by side in the garden.
Songs of crickets rise in silver bodies
under the v of geese returning to the lake.
The once burst-open blooms close their petals slowly.
Inside them lie memories of butterflies sipping.

LONIDIER RAMPANT

As from a distance, watch yourself
Disintegrate in foaming seas.
                        —Weldon Kees

You are too near the bridge
To have such hair
Hair a man would love
To comb his fingers through
Lonidier

Walking down the old familiar street
Doorways reappear
Shoe Repair New Soles
Smell of polish and leather
Where you sat in a chair
Swinging bobby soxed feet
Lonidier

Salvation waits on the corner of doughnut holes
Six to a bag
And in Mr. Bay's barber chair
Platinum bangs feathered on the floor
Lonidier

The bridge *Lonidier* and the sea *Lonidier*
And the dark morning hours
Chew through your brain
Looking for innocence
Lost *Lonidier*

And the stab in your heart where the intersection
Of life and death is marked

Cool fingers of fog have been waiting
All these years
Lonidier
Knowing one day you'd be theirs

You are too near the bridge
To have such hair
So you'll cut it off
Leave its stories behind
Or if they stay
Whispering in the roots
You'll feel it pulled by the updraft
Of love you left behind
Wasted
Unbelieved
Lonidier   Your hair
Will be the last of you
To hit the sea
The city that saved you again and again
Rising swiftly
To still you
To sleep

———————————————————————

Note: The poet Lynn Lonidier committed suicide by
jumping off a cliff in San Francisco. The woman in this
poem considers the Golden Gate Bridge.

ASHES

On the day she told us
the cancer had spread
to bone and brain we
went to the car where
once you were seated
i asked where do you
want to go, then said
i'd take you anywhere
today i did the same
put you inside the car,
strapped you in, then,
with my hand on the
velvet bag that held
the urn of your body
asked where do you
want to go and knew
before it was out of
my mouth completely
you were already there
that i was the only
lost one, wondering
now what, where?

FIELD SONG

Disappeared in darkness the trees
stand loudly in the night

Crickets quick-pulse brightly
between stars of twirled nests
and the glass-lined dwelling

From the redwood
the owl's long soft trill
on the exhale

Insects, birds and angels
call together as if
our frail beauty
matters not at all

FAREWELL SONG
for the ashes of Frank Decot

The wind traveled to my ear
leaf to leaf
It told the world *hush* —
here is grief

The trees stood as swaying ghosts
bough to bough
I lay upon their roots'
damp green vow

Their braided fingers held me
up for light
I slept outside their hollows —
cruel-ribbed night

In the morning there appeared —
lest I run —
quills of gold sensations,
spears of sun

shining a naked ribbon —
a prism found!
More ravishing than death
Spring's reflective gown

       Today, May, I will be a bird, red-eyed and free
       to fly over the long body of water where
       waves blown and bare
       blend ash to silver —
       fling him
           into air

THE HATED RELATION

The death smell is sweet...mostly with cancer patients.
— b.j.

Everyone hates him.
The way he just appears
out of the black berserk,
invades your body at once

or stays, as Miles put it,
local as a motherfucker —
breast, pancreas, colon, lung,
etcetera

He slams you to your atheist knees
begging for a miracle. Prayers
tear up from the brink as he
unmakes you and unmakes you.

The impossible blue sky
becomes a dark mosque of song,
an upturned cask of shadow.

The hated relation doesn't bother to pack or unpack.
He's here and then on to the next and the next.
If he says winter is in spring or summer, he's right.
In the end, he smells much sweeter than he is.

EL VIENTO EN SANTA ROSA

está el mismo del amor —
constante con sus rotaciones
en temperatura,
la dirección —
pero allí está.
Lo siento la —
en el forsythia temblante,
en el cielo bajo
con su cordon goteando —
está allí
en el perro dormiendo
inconsciente
de su muerte
o de la muerte
de su hombre

THE WIND IN SANTA ROSA

is the same as love —
constant with its shifts
in temperature and direction —
but it is there. I feel it —
in the trembling forsythia,
in the low sky with its
dripping lace —
it is there
in the dog sleeping
unaware of her death
or the death
of her man

MOTHER,

in a waitress uniform,
in a pancake house,
in the eye of sailors peering

Mother, dark of eye and ground, grand
daughter of Absolom,
blood of Sytha,

left so many times
you learned little of loving
but leaving

> *She was drunk*
> *She fell from the window*
> *Her foot caught between two pipes*
> *hung by broken bones*
> *He wouldn't let the children use the phone*

> *She was drunk*
> *She lit the match*
> *The water heater exploded*
> *burned her hair and lashes*
> *O how she cried on the floor!*
> *He wouldn't get up from his chair*

Every child cometh from darkness —
small open force unhidden —
Light transfers from the formless,
smatters across the given
world
And what of the mother who
chose not a boy or a girl
but *fun* before the breakthrough?

Mother of freckled arms and white ponies
fog glazes your eyes
Weighed down hard you hum the song,
and through prison bars of *home*
tell your children *no matter*
what you do, my dear, my dear,
don't have children

      Thus, naked among green and white
      blowing foam, they slept,
      faces on elbows, elbows on grass,
      inches from barnacle-covered steps
      leading to starfish tender in their rhythms,
      until the sun rose like the mother of all flowers
      burning on the green

      no matter what you do

      don't

      *

PÓRTICO

This porch isn't really a porch but a stoop
of old cement, a steady rope of ants between
step and riser making its way to a mystery
that just yesterday smelled like something rotting
and today has no smell at all. Twice I've told people
die and meant it. Grandma Torrez spent three
comatose days draped with clinging familia. *Just
go, Abuela. They'll live.*

Roses are lined up like laborers in the heat or hems
of Woolworth's aprons. Some are wound tight in
jalapeño-green wraps, others unfold petal by petal
on their way to becoming nothing. Their scents
fuse in the breeze and arrive as one: *Rosa.* From
slavery and Mexico without a patch of ground to the
Hills Brothers factory, she found it possible then
to buy a house with a porch on Geneva Avenue.

The mockingbird is trying to fool every dove, finch,
and warbler in the neighborhood. Do they fall for it?
She wasn't really my grandmother but a brutal
lover's. After I left him she let me live behind a
curtain in her garage, taught me a little español,
cooked me menudo y tamales dulces. She was the
only grandmother I ever had. I told her to die.
        ¡Le dije morir! And it worked.

BIRD. SONG. KNIFE. HEART.

> There are no ways of love but beautiful
>
> Lenore Kandel

for Robin

Morning's azure door opens
to daytime dream states
   Citrus, Camellia
   Bird of Paradise reaching

Stars related to water   to wind
fade with soft petal avalanche
   Ssshhhhhh

Abandoned by words and energy
to place one next to another
a green dream memory
leans against the wall
— invisible presence speaking

     Bird /Song
     Knife/Heart

Robin laid down in the sober creation
of women   chanted from the customs book
    (On the first day scissors)
Hair twined around fingers
pain
   lessly   like a birdwing
      snipped

Pat and Ruth
Skye and Snake
Phyllis and Del
living *together!*
Laughter   Dancing

Swans
      wings open
  dipped in women's light

10 years   20 years   35 years   together!

Not even a star
fallen like a sparrow
could be as alone
if she were to lose faith in me

It felt   Safe
It felt   Family   as
Billy Graham   had once
      Just as I am I come to thee

They became Wife and Wife   Two tendrils braided

Song of our bodies' shimmer
Song of fingers in familiar paths
Soft pant nibble the long O
O and O two bodies flowing
four breasts Bird and air and fury!

Your lips   my bride O
drip honey. The scent of your
clothing is the scent of Lesbiana

Knife/Heart
See the lonely blossoms grow apart
    Time ticking its circle of pain
      apart   apart

In the thirteenth year
a folkdance class
   a man
            intoxication
She let go   let go
      His fingertips   his mouth

> *The down-turned blooms of the trumpet vine*
> *pressed yellow against the wall*
>   *wake side-by-side*
>   *in the garden of near silent songs*

> *Flutes and buds among shadow-play*
> *shake from the soft bee's buzz –*
>   *a roar in their petals*
>   *dropping like garments   one by one*

> *Combustible flowers hanging mutely*
> *there are two who know you*
>   *in your curves and cries*
>   *your throats no different from their own –*

>   *so close to birds – veiled –*
>   *hearts nailed to the mist-drenched morning*

Something familiar   a language
      between them   Whispered
Songs passed from mouth to mouth   limb to limb swirling
          ballads
             lullabies
                The Wooing Song

> *While in his leaves there shrouded lay*
> *Sweet birds, for love that dance and play*

She fell and fell

>   *want*
>   felt in the middle
>   *want*
>   inside the throat
>   *want*
>   arms pushed out
>   *want*
>   back arched back
>   spell-notched
>   (receiving)

His words were the equivalent of stars
They danced entire constellations

>   *apart   apart*

Blank passion   through her eyes
confessed one night
after her Wife had eaten
>   *loneliness   longing and lack*
Gross bitch! Lesbiana replied   *OUT!*
>   *Go on, go on, thou false one! now*
>   *Upon his shoulder rest thy brow,*
>   *And look into his eyes until*
>   *Thine own,*
>>   *to find them colder,*
>>>   *fill.*

He couldn't leave his children, his
wife

There is love and there is
deadly love   picking the locks
of the heart's solid building
under a moon turned to bone

That's life! said Lesbiana,
satisfied

Backs turned on the backslider
moonscapes of muscles
unmoving

> *lake edge wind*
> *snake ripples blown*
> *side long*
> *against the shore*
> *cormorants*
> *bench plaque*
> *caterpillar's end of world =*
> *Mother's butterfly*
> *when virginia entered*
> *when crane and kees*
> *when lonidier*
> *leapt to the sea*
> *what bridge*
> *waited there*
> *what cocoon*

> *what wings?*

once
in a born-again time
after a night of demons
she determined the cause
was saying the lord's prayer
backwards

discovered
live
spelled backwards
is *evil*

what wings?

She lay down
with her pills
and died
(*Dry drunk!* they cried. *Sex
killed her*)

Alone
Extinguished
Brown-eyed Robin

> *They did not love me living; but once dead*

> *I will walk only when not bid to, arise*
> *from my bed of nothing, my hair of time*
> *falling to the shoulder of space.*
> *If I speak, and I will only speak if not spoken to,*
> *I will have learned my words yesterday*
> *and will forget them tomorrow.*

As she lay
the loss of childhood
was added to the loss
of love

No one held her pretty hand
No one brushed her dark hair from her whitened face
No one saw her glide among the lake or river
a radiance wrapped in flame
No
She didn't grow to an Amazon's height
elusively out of the mists
or hover over the law-full hills of Lesbiana

> *Skin was shed and an angel stood there*
> *capable of every form — beyond*
> *the human border*

Impossible to stop it

Her body
> *the upper half   sky*
> > *the lower half   earth*
> > > *from her water came forth clouds*
> > > > *her tears the source*
> > > > > *of our rivers*
> > > > > > *and our dreams*

Heart!

      O

            Heart

CONTINENT OF LIGHT

UFFIZI

Square blocks of light
        path in and out of shadow
Frosted windows, women of clean,
        cold marble. (What would be the use
of getting to know each other?) White
        shoulders, white
necks, white
        empty eyes

The maiden look (your eyes on me)
                dismembered.
To lean toward the nude torso – white
        shaft of sunlight
striking from the back, armless,
        (defenseless as a girl)
a new view of the world   – fragmented –
        (What would be the use?)

A simple breast lends grace
        to stone. Ivory skull. Closed face.
(Like a flower shut tight)
One hand under a chin (your smile was a corpse),
        the other at an ear (and then, lessons)
heart encased in rock (a scar) or

floated down the lightshaft
(love deceives) to skin before the sun falls
   into darkness (your mouth). What dwells there?
(Steam. The blueness of a river.)

IN A HOUSE BENEATH DEEP RED LEAVES

a woman with a moon in her chest
sings like a cricket freed from her cage.

All of her dreams enter at an angle
from an unfamiliar city. They moisten her skin.

From her window she feels the slow surrender
of roses to heat, their opening to light.

She has no longing for spring, just for the slow
moving day to reach the open furrows

where night seeds are planted,
for that warmest moment just before waking.

ELYSIAN

The golden field
  the merging streams
      their love-love duet
muting voluptuously
  the world's slow turn
      beneath the breathless sky

All sense of direction
    gladly lost   borrowed bird song
        rising and falling
gold chorus of sighs   grass
    like hair   tree and time
        suddenly hallowed   glittering

All of nature come
    to the sweet nothing
        this side of the stone wall
transfigured by the silent
    bursting

CONTINENT OF LIGHT

The No Angel walks from slivered
daymoon to child sea —
yellow trumpet vines drape stucco walls,
shock against a brilliant sky —
        every syllable enters her eyes

Water birds of pleasure and cupped cloudbursts
glide into the port of longing,
long curved pier of dreams —

        landscape of starfish rearranging their arms
        armor plated barnacles cemented head first
        on steps descending

Love potion of breeze and half-eaten sky,
double note of fog,
lead to evening's paneless window,
white-scarfed reach of sea

        a small sleeve of flowers wanted tears
        but they were with the fishing boat —
        chugging away

A cover is needed
to keep the light
from the eye

Sometimes it's a lie
Love is neither sea nor concrete
but mathematics — multiplication,
subtraction. (How many were there then —
Brittle Stars, Pink stars, Six-rayed, Bats?)

The walls are covered with it —
wood and glass and grain,
doors held open with little more than a hip
or kicked shut

     Carried home in protective pockets the stars
     died slowly

How does one let go of love?
    A sketched Mastodon is as easily erased
    as a hummingbird   or
    a hummingbird is as difficult to wipe out
    as a Mastodon.

     Where is the shore of your dream,
     little boat drifting
     to crystal fiddles?

The port is a mouth —
blue bed against
a brick wall

The No Angel remembers kisses (they sit together)
the only ones to survive (having perished) when
sea birds V west to east, east to west,
wings tilted (free!) against the world

She lies on her back
    Mossy steps of stars
counting each new light
    under the rhyming sea
trusting they'll last a while

RATS

A Poem of Jealousy

The rats always arrived the same day
the other woman walked though the door
As she kissed his cheek, his mouth, his lips,
as he brushed his hand across her breasts,

the rats scurried madly across the floor
The rats followed them to bed, their tiny
front paws with their needle-like claws
propped up on the edge, their eyes

were onyx teardrops
Their sharp teeth chewed and chewed
until the bed was gone, the floor was gone,
the whole room falling through,

crashing, breaking into splinters
The rats lay exhausted around the jagged
edges, their filthy bodies spelling
love

SEISMOLOGY

The moon doesn't show its face in the city
and so we guess how to behave; whether
to give in to love again, howl our pain,
or hide under the cold bed where darkness

thumps its Olympian skull. The old hotel
sits on abandoned ships with sealed bottles
of champagne, their captains gone off for gold
that never panned out. Our wish

is just for ground to act like ground again,
to hold us firmer than fog, than water,
for the moon to break through and knock us down,
tell us what to do with these shaken ruins.

Without Self-Pity We Wouldn't Have Popular Songs

I'm sitting on a park bench, wild
blackberries weighing to the ground,

each bloodied anchor sweet in the rotting
sun. The moon bloats in the blue sky, hungry

for this vacancy to fill, this howitzer shell of a day
without you, the history of us undone.

To the north the first star emits an odor of rusting
ploughs and a bird sings a song quickly —

quickly forgotten and my toe digs in the ground searching
for every lost minute. My single love. This is where

age comes in handy. The end of black-and-white
thinking. The knowing we'll stumble back again,

this day a shadow gobbled by a horde of unfinished
dreams making themselves as real as my desire

to fly backwards. Sometimes we laugh
when we make love. Remember?

Twister

Our new home was enormous on its Georgia plot
where bugs bigger than peach pits dropped
out of trees to land in our dresses and the clay
still smacked of blood and we-shall-rise-again.
In winter, cardinals perched in fruitless pears
as the cake-toting curious inquired in minor chords

not our names but first where we're from and second
just which church we attend. Come summer,
downpours soaked the yards in white-capped waves
five hours from the sea and I learned to drop the phone
when thunder clapped, the windows flooding with
alternating light and dark. Once we heard a train roaring

down our trackless road. It elevated and twisted, not
bending the trees but snapping them at an even seven feet.
We couldn't see any of this crammed into the bunker of the
half bath beneath the stairs, clinging to news like kudzu,
the matter-of-fact tone on our battery-operated radio flattening
everything between the whining and whistling of the cracking

crashing world into a flapping map of road winding through
Tennessee, ending back in California where we drove all packed
through lolling parched and burnished hills basking
in the breathless sun, cows lumbering a slow migration
to pools of oak-leafed shade, horses in the plain dozing
to highway hum, not even a fly to shoo, the only roar more

a whisper of plane soaring over the hay-sweet vista, its vapor trail
anchored in a clear blue prophecy: earthquake weather.

BREATHING

Jack London State Park

This is where it is done. Beneath the canopy
of trees above and the many songbirds
we've not had time to learn the names of
by their chips and trills, here where bees effervesce
in gold light, water still spilling on the rocks,
and inside the softly carpeted fairy ring

where braided shadows of redwoods drape
nests of mice, voles. Breath comes more softly
standing at the picket fence of graves —
London under the red rock, fresh ashes
poured in a mound nearby. (We wondered if
that's desecration or a human right.) It comes

deeper in the garden of rosemary, lavender,
and quicker at the cottage when we realize
the woodpeckers will win in the end with
no one to mend the walls. Dear Jack: I like
peeking in the windows to see your desk,
your books, your sleeping porch and Charmian's

where you were brought to die, but mostly
I like to walk the land left to us. Is there
anything you can do from where you are? Be
a hero. Send a ship or a good dog. Think
Wolf House. Happy House. This restful,
delicious house of air. We breathe here
better than almost anywhere, distressed.

White Horse

Through the woods of Annadel,
past trees gently arched,
trunks and stones moss-matted —
comes the fair stallion steady on the trail

One angel on a treetop sings
one note, repeated,
repeated

Milky surface of stream,
little wall of water
falling into it,
and the white horse
coming nearer
with a steady sound
beating under the boughs
in the darkness of woods
as if by magic
moving towards
to where, upon the ribbed edge,
he passes
trails a veil of light
that shakes us
      as though wind
      as though ecstasy

ONCE UPON A TIME IN ANNADEL

We were as rivulets in rain-awakened woods
Beneath the grand arch of limbs we wandered
furred with green.   It was all about moss
and moisture then, the living spirit of the frame,
ribbed and branching. Among the singing sweep
we sensed the deep of it, the entrance
to another world, a larger art where even
the biggest horse was but a fairy transport.
We had fantasies and hope as our mortal
muscles moved past cats and quails, spice bush,
monkey flowers, three riders on three
Norwegian Fjords. The countdown to closure
had stopped in place. There were fox dens and snake caves
and a woman running with perfume and pearls, but no
blotting out, no grave for this light, this life.

    And then — just because —
    a picnic bench. Silence,
    sealed and secret.

THE DEEP

Beneath fresh green leaves
        within the wind's silver fingers
a dream

Bodies deep in clockless clouds
        Waterfall-mimicry —
                endless
                        attainable

Invisible birds sweetly
        singing, budding
where beasts lie, where breasts

of bright plumes among honeycombs,
        sylvan echoes

tease the brightness
        Changing light — butter-yellow temple

of a i r,

        maps of deep red
immortal reel

flesh back to flower
        seed and seedlette
Scent
        Scent

Eyelid-shutter — Disobedience
bellowing *radiance*

A dance to the tune
      of black angels
strawed and streamed — Macaw-bright
unbound, free
      Difference
Metallic sea bobbing
Ribbons of night fanning dreams
      wound through rustling wilderness

Darkness, and its strange end

Unforgotten beauty — silent rain-feathers
upon the unshed

    t

     e

      a

       r

        s

O Dark
     O Darkness

Beneath the murmuring horizon
     your ghostly gown coiling 'round
sailors lost —
     vacant quench

Our bond —
Our black-winged song —
Our youth-dew come
     again

        Life
        u n c a g e d!

Sidhe

SIDHE

for Jack Foley

[Sidhe, pronounced SHE, means a people of the hills. It is the Gaelic
name for fairies. Descended from people defeated in war, the Sidhe
retreated to a different dimension of space and time. They have the
power to move quickly through air and change their shape at will. The
Sidhe live under mounds. The Sidhe in this poem live in San Francisco.]

Shape-shifters
        Earth walkers
                Night flyers

                Dwellers under the hills
        Ireland/SanFrancisco
                (there)   (there)

AN O'SIDHE IS BORN IN THE FLATLANDS

My mother was of Ireland,
      My father came to dance…

The father 9 months later   *Love like heat and cold*
moves down the street   *Pierces and then is gone;*
with Bernadine Of the Tight Maroon Dress
     Jealousy when it strikes
and Large Bosom.   *Sticks in the marrowbone*

     Here's health to your enemy's enemies

Father O'Bank O'American Dream
New Cars   *Here's health and prosperity*
For the girls new matching dresses
     to you and all your posterity
New shoes
New, New, O'New! O'New!   *damned for all eternity*

New bank examiner, new
trial, new word:
Embezzlement

What did the Bank Examiner say to the father of O'Sidhe?
Go to jail.

What did the Bank Examiner say to the mother of O'Sidhe
Marry me.

Here's to you and yours and to mine and ours and if

AFTER A SMALL WEDDING WHICH SHE DIDN'T ATTEND,
O'SIDHE IS BANISHED TO THE HILLS

Yellow Mercury green
        interior Lucky Strikes
Closed windows   *May the road rise to meet you*
        600 miles northward northward northward
looking at the back of the head
        of the Mortal Son of Un-nourishing Substance
          "Who Is He?
                Open the door I'm going to be sick."

Bottom of a hill. Curbside. Sunlight
        limping through the fog.
Six steps to the locked door.
        More steps. *May peace and plenty*
Up. Up. *be the first to lift the latch*

Here's your room. Good-bye.

BIRDSEED

What the Mortal Son
          of Un-nourishing Substance calls it.
    Lithium   Valium   Seconal cradled
palm of hand
          bourbon swirling
Head back re-fills
          spits "I hate the sight of you!"
O'Sidhe is five, still wondering
who is he, the cockalorum

O Little O'Sidhe, how is your heart now?

How to Go Invisible: Get a raven's heart, split
it open with a black hafted knife, make three
cuts, place a black bean in each cut. Plant it.
When the beans sprout put one in your mouth,
say "By virtue of Satan's heart, by strength of
my great art, I desire to be invisible." So it will
be as long as the bean is kept in the mouth."

And the Flower Like Milk in a Dark Pantry At Night

Narrow hallway   Pantry   The Mortal Man
       of Un-Nourishing Substance
reaches for O'Sidhe

I see the color on your head but
What color is your hair
Really?

O'Sidhe perches high in the corner
back pushed against the ceiling.
Fi! Fie! Fo! Fum!
She didn't know
Flight
until he came — the Mortal Son.
O'Mind! O'Powerful Mind!
No man can reach the shape-shifter.

I could scale the blue air
I could plough the high hills
I could kneel at night in prayer
To heal your many ills

white of the washer and dryer
or the way the step-girls tossed

their panties in, slammed shut the lid
instead of leaving them to soak
in the bathroom basin, instead

of hanging them to dry over the
curtain rod. He missed walking
into the green-tiled room, fingering

the delicate pink skin of them
as they dripped at his feet. He sidles
through the empty house looking for

something. Sunlight fires from a mirror. Young
again, he turns, sees his father standing with a gun
to his head. We all see ancestors

in the mirror. And then the pink
foam and the bits of brain
and the pink rag plunged

again and again into the mucky pail.
The clock strikes three. The girls
will soon be home. He sits waiting,

his memory a silverfish gone to black,
he sits waiting, craving
one tender thing.

WHERE O'SIDHE KEEPS HER TONGUE

In a silver box
shaped like a shield, a spear.

Evenings, she slips it
from safety, sings to her sister
songs of stars and moon.

Before sleep she plucks it,
returns it to the vault
of silent daughters.

O'SIDHE OF GREENWICH STREET

Twenty-one-eighty-two is the color of dirty Caucasian flesh.
Squint your eyes: Dead doves of tissue float from the
landlord's room, rest on heads of passing schoolgirls.
Rocking to and fro he whistles one long strain.
Phantom train in the night, long forgotten teapot.
He giggles like a girl.

Twenty-one-eighty-two, stairs burrow under to the dirt-
walled cellar where the Mortal Man, the step-man,
mounts the whimpering stairs. Hair wrapped around fist,
feet dangling down the hall, a garbage sack of a Sidhe
is tossed, door slammed shut. She'd been off the block
again. Was missing. Was found.

Upstairs the teapot, downstairs the dungeon,
in between
moonlight pulled over song.

Twenty-one-eighty-two, through the keyhole waft of cow's
tongue, delusion tinkling on ice. The parakeet bangs his head
against his little bell, hangs on the unforgiving hook.
Up the sun-drenched block from

twenty-one-eighty-two O'Sidhe finds comfort hugging concrete,
chanting safety over ants. Walking home the windows of
Greenwich Street flare. With one hand she catches a dove,
breathes it back to flight, with the other
turns the sizzling knob.

YELLOW DRESS

Home below the hill
papered with air
brushed skin.   *Fairies are said to be beautiful*
                        with long yellow hair
Women imperfectly hairless
There   *and delicate forms*

No wounds from the war
on women. *They have the power to affect human life*
They are hungry and O'Sidhe
learns the lesson
and she hungers   *often luring mortals*
and she is alone
hungering.   *into an eternal dance*

Bare shoulder on the screen   *May your body not cease*
bare white shoulder   *to pay me attention*
strap slipping down   *may your love follow my face*
the yellow dress on the floor
                        as the cow follows her calf

all help

(Fleshswell!)

but not enough.

O John Wayne
Why did you burst through that
door?

O'SIDHE RENTS A WEDDING DRESS

Temporary
Light tilting through window
impaled   frigid sheets
Lonely

Give me more love or more disdain

He knows purity   *The torrid, or the frozen zone*
but not the body   *Either extreme, of love, or hate,*
Unresponsive flesh.   *Is sweeter than a calm estate.*
House of gallows

She leaves the flatlands,   *Farewell love*
snowfields,
for the bottom of the hill.   *and thy laws forever*
Fillmore. Greenwich.
Called
The Bermuda Triangle.   *Thy baited hooks*
People vaporize
legs open   *tangle me no more*
to the imperfect.

An O'Sidhe Bleeds On the Street

from the tooth   *Hearts blood*
the hombre has left   *and bowel's blood*
a window calls the cops   *May your eyes go blind*
her hair is long, the color   *And your knees be broken!*
of moon
so they will ride the hills
searching
She says Let him go   *And no man in Ireland*
                            will fire the shot
he's just an hombre

O'Sidhe comes through the fog
to live in a car.
It's warm
most days.

O'SIDHE LIVES THROUGH

The women's hot tub
a block from the ocean.
Clothes in trees.
Naked back and forth
across the Great Highway.
One man disappears,   *arms extended like a cross*
morning is wrapped in a sheet   *without a sound*
from someone's line.   *the lost are found!*

Booze   weed   'shrooms   *Angel of this sacred place*
sometimes more
than she bargains for.
                    Calm her soul and whisper peace

Twin Peaks Woman
undresses in front of the fire
undresses O'Sidhe, too.
(O John Wayne stay away
from the shape-shifter!)
A man she thinks she loves
and comes hard to   *Night flyer*
but she is Irish (remember?)
and he is Jewish so,
you know,
the Mother.   *Earth Walker*

Then coke   then dope   *Shape shifter*
then Death with a capital D
one night standing   *Night flyer*
right in the corner

the 80s pounding on the door   *Earth!*
screaming
WAKE UP! EVERYONE'S GOING
STRAIGHT!   *Night!*

She didn't.   *Flyer!*

Away, come away:
Empty your heart of its mortal dream.

O, Dark mother

Coda

WHITTENBERG

Along the trail that climbs up to sky
birdsongs weave through a revel of leaves.
Their notes hover in shadowed stories high
above winter's falls, within the heart's grief

to come. I have loved the world for this
kindness that presents as if from a dream.
My forest of silence and scent and bliss —
you ease all sorrows a human life brings.

In full sun I lay across your needled path,
draw over my body a cloak of pine.
The motion of trees renews my faith
in enchantment everywhere within your eye.

To mingle with moss and this forest's breath
is to grow back to a child's taintless
view of nature-power and perfect wealth.
Such magic in the lone hours, in stillness,

the whole day anchored in a sweet-breath bed
where voices of trees, wrens and ground all blend
amid the spread of angels crowned with green.
Your atmosphere of light invades, reshapes me.

CLOUDS

The sound of her beauty enters my body

My body cannot refuse the stranger
            known for millennia

Or turn from the city of dreams
Where fog and light
Pierce
Breast through back

            World on its axis

Two red tailed hawks drift over the valley
            Coyotes sing from the hills

In fog you are everywhere
            and nowhere

Mist and light swirl in faerie dust
            Out of it, like a magician, comes…

ACKNOWLEDGEMENTS

Thanks to CJ Rayhill for the love, encouragement and gift of time that make a life of writing possible; to the dozens of poets who have offered inspiration and encouragement; to Jack Foley for suggesting the title "Without Self-Pity We Wouldn't Have Popular Songs".

I also wish to thank the editors of the following publications in which some of these poems first appeared: *The Book of Forms — A Handbook of* Poetics (University Press of New England, Lewis Putnam Turco, ed.); *Visions & Affiliations — A California Literary Timeline* (Pantograph Press, Jack Foley, ed.); *Updraft* (Finishing Line Press); *Ahadada Reader 3,* (Ahadada Press).

Additional thanks go to the editors of the following literary publications and journals: *Ambush Review; Beatitude; Comstock Review; Golden Handcuffs Review; New College Review; Parthenon West Review;* and *The Sow's Ear.*

KATHERINE HASTINGS grew up in the Cow Hollow neighborhood of San Francisco. Her poems have been published widely in journals and anthologies. Chapbooks published are *Fog and Light* (Ahadada Reader 3, Ahadada Press 2011); and *Updraft* (Finishing Line Press, 2010). She is the host of *WordTemple* on NPR affiliate KRCB FM and curator of the WordTemple Poetry Series in Sonoma County, CA. Her Small Change Series of WordTemple Press has published beat poet David Meltzer, San Francisco poet laureate emerita devorah major, and many others, as well as the anthology *What Redwoods Know — Poems from California State Parks* (all proceeds go to the California State Parks Foundation). She lives in Sonoma County with her partner, CJ Rayhill and Chihuahua, Gizmo Federíco Garcia Lorca. For more information go to www. wordtemple.com.

S P U Y T E N   D U Y V I L

Meeting Eyes Bindery
Triton
Lithic Scatter

www.ingramcontent.com/pod-product-compliance
Lightning Source LLC
Chambersburg PA
CBHW020921090426
42736CB00008B/734